Stylish Pieces with
Embossed Metal
Textured Mesh
Beads
and Wire

by Linda Peterson

Metal Jewelry 101

Creating fashionable metal and wire jewelry is easy, enjoyable and requires only inexpensive tools. In no time at all you will find yourself working with aluminum, copper and pewter to fashion accessories that coordinate beautifully with your wardrobe.

As you become more familiar with the metals, advance to creating faux surfaces like enamel. These designs are perfect focal pieces for existing beaded necklaces you may already have in your jewelry collection. Why not give an old piece a new, trendy look? Watch the discount jewelry stores for inexpensive beaded necklaces suitable for embellishing with your unique style.

Once your creative juices are really flowing, try working with Rubber Stamps. You can't make a mistake! Use the designs in this book as a jump start. Remember this style isn't supposed to be perfect. Consider using found objects to give your design that one-of-a-kind natural look.

So jump in, create, have fun and play! Be confident that your friends and family will admire your jewelry!

Basic Supplies

Clear Stencil plastic (thick and thin) • Texturing materials (texture sheets, plastic Aida cloth, anything that can go through the pasta machine and create a texture) Pasta machine • Craft foam • Pliers • Liver of Sulfur • Glass or plastic bowls Rubbing alcohol • Wipes • Baking soda • Rubber stamps • Scissors • Hammer Wooden stylus • Toothpicks • Wire cutters • Heat gun • Epoxy glue • Super pink tape

Basic Jewelry Tools

Round-nose pliers • Jump rings • Silver spacers • Toggles Clasps • Leather cording • Silver wire • FunWire

Basics in Working with Metals

Use caution when working with metals as the edges are very sharp and can cause injury. These projects are not recommended for small children.

Generally the metal can be cut with common household scissors. To prepare metals, lightly sand the surface and clean with rubbing alcohol to remove any oily residue. You can then apply one or more surface techniques such as stamping with ink designed specifically for metal.

The metal can be texturized in a variety of ways from using a metal stylus to create a design or by working with texture plates and a pasta machine. It can also be stamped using inks that are designed for metals.

Copper is one of the most versatile metals in the ArtEmboss line. It can be heated to achieve a variety of colors beginning from a burnt-golden orange to purples and blues. Make sure that you protect your hands while heating as the copper gets extremely hot. Use pliers to pick up and hold the metal.

Copper will also distress when dipped into liver of sulfur solution. Many of the projects featured use this technique.

Aluminum metals are thinner and some are even color coated. These too can be stamped or texturized. Since the color is a topical surface, you can distress the metal by light sanding.

As with any craft project, proper tools and proper handling of the materials are necessary to achieve good results. To prevent injury, please use care when working with the different solutions and metals.

TIP: To prevent double stick tape from sticking to scissors when cutting objects out, apply a very thin layer of petroleum jelly to the unwanted tape and to the scissors. Any residue that remains can be cleaned up with rubbing alcohol.

Design Originals

For a color catalog featuring over 200 terrific 'How-To' books, **visit www.d-originals.com**

© 2009 DESIGN ORIGINALS by *Suzanne McNeill*, 2425 Cullen St, Fort Worth, Texas 76107, U.S.A., 817-877-0067 • www.d-originals.com

Silver - Blue - Purple Earrings

Thoroughly modern and totally trendy, these colorful layered creations are only limited by your imagination. Layer your earrings with different colors and textures. Cut random shapes from leftover pieces of plastic and metal.

SIZE: Beaded: ⅞" x 2"
Square: ¾" x ¾"

MATERIALS:
ArtEmboss (Violet, Cerulean Blue) • Clear stencil plastic • Piñata alcohol ink (Blues, Purples) • Rubbing Alcohol in spray bottle • Make up sponges • 2 head pins • Jump rings • Ear wires • Silver non-tarnish wire • Beads (2 Violet 3mm faceted, 2 Silver 2mm round spacer) • Sanding sponge • ¹⁄₁₆" round punch • Double-sided tape • 3-D Zot Dot • 2 part epoxy glue

INSTRUCTIONS:
Beaded Earrings: Using pattern, cut out stencil plastic for both shapes. Apply tape and Silver metal to both sides of the larger background piece. Tape Violet metal to one side of the small upper layer piece. • Daub Silver pieces with alcohol ink. Spritz with rubbing alcohol to mottle. Lightly sand all edges. Emboss detail if desired. • Punch a hole in the bottom layer for attaching ear wires. Adhere top piece to bottom with Zot dot. Create a metal embellishment with a piece of wire 1½" long. Form a loop at one end, zig zag and finish with coil. Attach ear wire and metal embellishment with jump ring. • Punch a hole in the bottom of the earring. Thread beads onto head pin. Create a loop and attach loop to bottom of earrings.

Square Earrings: Using pattern, cut out stencil plastic for both shapes. Apply tape and Blue metal to both sides of square. Tape Silver metal to both sides of the triangle. • Daub Blue pieces with alcohol ink. Spritz with rubbing alcohol to mottle. Lightly sand all edges. Emboss detail if desired. • Glue Silver triangle, metal swirl and rhinestone to the background square. Punch a hole in the triangle and attach ear wires.

Copper - Silver Earrings

Perfect for that little black dress or blue jeans, the shimmer of silver and copper add sparkle to your day and sizzle in the evening.

SIZE: ⅝" x 1⅝"

MATERIALS:
ArtEmboss (Copper Light, Aluminum) • Clear stencil plastic • Jump rings • Earring wires • ¹⁄₁₆" round hole punch • Double-sided tape

INSTRUCTIONS:
Top layer: Cut stencil plastic 2" x 2½". Cover with tape. • Cut a piece of each metal 1" x 2½". Using a ruler, mark off ¼" strips. Cut strips of each color of metal ¼" x 2½". Lay side by side onto tape. Cut strips in the opposite direction ¼" x 1¼".

Bottom layer: From plastic cut ⅝" x 1⅝". Cover with tape and Copper. Cut a strip of Silver ⅜" x 1½" and tape to Copper piece.
Finish: Punch a hole in the top of each layer. Attach layers with a jump ring. Attach an ear wire.

Copper - Silver Earrings
1. Apply tape to template plastic. • 2. Score lines on the metal ¼" apart. • 3. Adhere strips to the template plastic.

 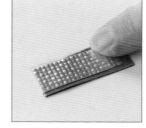

4. Cut striped strips. • 5. Adhere Silver to the Copper bottom layer.

Create Beautiful Lightweight Earrings to Wear with Everything!

CREATING TEXTURE AND COLOR ON METAL

Paper punches come in various shapes and sizes and are perfect to create metal jewelry quickly and easily. I lean more towards basic geometric shapes that can be combined in a variety of ways for stunning, easy-to-create designs.

Combining these shapes with all the new trendy findings makes designing jewelry a snap!

Around the World Jewelry

It's a blue planet, but feel free to color your world to match your favorite outfit or your mood. The silver chain and outer ring complement everything in your wardrobe.

SIZE: Necklace 19", Earrings 1¼"

MATERIALS:
ArtEmboss Seafoam Green Aluminum • Plastic Aida cloth • Pasta machine • Craft foam • Clear stencil plastic • Silver Leaf Rub 'n Buff • Jump rings (three ½", eight ¼") • Silver hoops (one 1½", two 1") • Clasp • 18" Silver chain • Sanding sponge • Round punches (1¼", ⅞", ⁵⁄₁₆", ¹⁄₁₆") • StrongARM punching helper • Double-sided tape

INSTRUCTIONS:

Prep: Texturize metal by rolling a sandwich of craft foam, metal and Aida cloth thru the second thinnest setting of the pasta machine. • Apply tape to stencil plastic. Tape textured metal to both sides.

Necklace: Punch a ⁵⁄₁₆" hole in the textured metal. With the hole at the top, punch a 1¼" circle surrounding the smaller hole. Lightly sand surface to expose pattern. Highlight the edges with Rub 'n Buff. • Punch a ¹⁄₁₆" hole for jump ring. Open a small jump ring and attach a large Silver hoop and a ½" closed jump ring. Close small jump ring. Add to chain with another small jump ring.

Round Earrings: Punch a ⁵⁄₁₆" hole in the textured metal. With the hole at the top, punch a ⁷⁄₈" circle surrounding the smaller hole. Lightly sand surface to expose pattern. Highlight the edges with Rub 'n Buff. • Punch a ¹⁄₁₆" hole for jump ring. Open a small jump ring and attach a small Silver hoop. Close jump ring. Add to ear wire with another small jump ring. Make 2.

Drop Earrings: Use the punched out circles as elements for long drop earrings. Cut a piece of Silver wire 1½" long. Loop both ends. Use a small jump ring to attach a metal circle and a large closed jump ring to the looped end of the dangle wire. Attach the other looped end of the dangle wire to an ear wire. Make 2.

1. Layer craft foam, metal and Aida cloth. • 2. Run through the pasta machine on the second smallest setting.

3. Punch a hole in the textured metal surrounding the small hole. • 4. Punch a tiny hole in the top for a jump ring.

5. Attach circle to Silver hoop with a jump ring.

Embellish with Fabulous Colors and Textures to Wear with Everything!

Fan Fair Necklace

Drenched in tropical ocean colors, this necklace is pleasingly light and wonderful to wear. Make a matching bracelet with a smaller chain.

SIZE: 17"

MATERIALS:
ArtEmboss Aluminum (Seafoam Green, Cerulean Blue) • Plastic Aida cloth • Texture Sheet • Pasta machine • Craft foam • Clear stencil plastic • Sunflower Yellow Piñata alcohol ink • Rubbing Alcohol in a spray bottle • Make up sponges • Jump rings • Clasp • Chain • Sanding sponge • Punches (1" square, 1/16" round, Corner rounder) • StrongARM punching tool • Double-sided tape

INSTRUCTIONS:
Texturize metal by rolling a sandwich of craft foam, metal and Aida cloth or a Texture Sheet through the second thinnest setting of the pasta machine. • Punch 9 squares of stencil plastic & round the corners. Apply tape to both sides. Tape metal to both sides and cut out flush with the plastic. • To mottle the color of metal, lightly daub on alcohol ink. Spritz with alcohol. Lightly sand surface to expose Silver metal, leaving the colored metal in the grooves. • Punch a 1/16" hole in the top center. Attach to chain with jump rings. Attach toggle to chain with jump rings.

1. Lightly daub alcohol ink onto metal.

2. Spritz the metal with alcohol.

Stamped Multi-Layered Metal Pendant

Eclectic modern art meets traditional shape for a trendy accessory with classic style.

SIZE: Necklace: 16", Pendant 1¾ x 1⅞"

MATERIALS:
ArtEmboss (Copper Light, Pewter) • Silver 22 gauge wire • Metal Stamp Art Black ultra ink pad • Rubber stamp • Asian coin • Stencil plastic • Chain • Jump rings • Wood stylus • Metal stylus • Heat gun • 1/16" hole punch • Double-sided tape • 2 part epoxy glue

INSTRUCTIONS:
Cut out triangle shape from stencil plastic and apply tape to one side. Lay Pewter metal over triangle and cut out leaving a 1/4" border. Fold edges to back and burnish with wooden stylus. Draw lines on 1 corner. Stamp a word on Copper. Heat set. Cut out shape. Tape to front of pendant. Cut excess metal from edges. • Cover the back with tape and Copper. Trim edges flush. • Punch 6 holes on one side and thread Silver craft wire through holes. Glue on coin and let dry. • Punch 2 holes in top center. Wrap wire thru holes and around chain loop. Attach to desired chain with jump rings.
As a variation, repeat this design, except smaller for coordinating earrings.

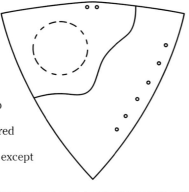

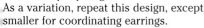

1. Burnish the edge on the back. • 2. Draw lines in one corner with a metal stylus. • 3. Stamp word on Copper shape. • 4. Adhere Copper and coin to triangle.

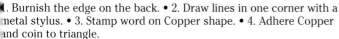

Copper Leaf Pendant and Earrings

Burnished copper leaves grace your wardrobe all year long with a beautiful organic look.

SIZE: Pendant: 1" x 3", Earrings: ¾" x 1¾"

MATERIALS:
ArtEmboss Copper Light • Thin brass rods • Rub 'n Buff (Black, Silver Leaf) • Copper Craft wire • 2 ear wires • Wooden stylus • 1⁄16" round hole punch • Makeup sponge • Steel wool • 2 part epoxy glue

INSTRUCTIONS:
Prep: Cut the following leaves from Copper using pattern: 1 each of #1 and #2 for pendant, 2 of #3 for earrings. Draw in vein marks with wooden stylus. Apply Black Rub 'n Buff to leaves with make up sponge. Let dry.

Gently buff off leaving Black in depressed areas. Apply Silver Rub 'n Buff around edges. • Punch holes as shown using in pattern.

Pendant: With brass rod, create a double-wrapped loop at one end. Trim to 2½". Shape into a wavy line and hammer flat. Secure to leaf #1 with Copper craft wire. Glue leaf #2 on top of leaf #1. Let dry.

Choker: Create a dip in the center of brass rods with pliers. Slip on leaf. Coil each end of the wire. Hammer flat. Cut another rod in half. Coil one end and loop the other. Hammer flat. • Create a hook clasp. • Attach each side piece to main center with 2 jump rings made from excess rods wrapped around a pencil.

Earrings: Cut 2" of wire. Turn a loop at one end. Shape the tail into a wavy line and hammer flat. Wire leaf to post through holes. Attach to ear wires.

1. Apply Rub 'n Buff to leaves. • 2. Form a double wrapped loop. • 3. Hammer the ends flat to make a support post. • 4. Use pattern to punch holes in Leaf #1. • 5. Wire the leaf to the support post.

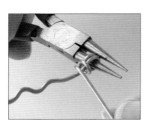

6. Curl the ends and shape a dip in the center of the choker wire. • 7. Curl the ends of the small pieces. • 8. Hammer the ends flat. • 9. Make jump rings: Wrap wire around a pencil. • 10. Remove curled wire and cut rings apart. • 11. Attach short piece of choker to main wire with 2 jump rings.

Victoriana Choker

Steeped in Victorian charm, this collage choker offers an entrancing collection of tiny decorative bits and pieces.

SIZE: Choker: 15", Pendant ⅞" x 1¾"

MATERIALS:
ArtEmboss (Copper medium, Pewter) • Copper 24 gauge craft wire • Liver of Sulfur • Baking soda • Steel wool • 220 grit sandpaper • 2 plastic or glass bowls • Water • Rubber stamp • Petroleum jelly • Clear acetate • Old photo • Assorted charms • Assorted beads • Jump rings • Head pin • Eye pins • Punches (1/16" round, Corner rounder) • Big Kick die cut machine (optional) with Sizzix ⅝" x ⅞" frame die • 2 part epoxy glue

INSTRUCTIONS:
Choker: Cut two 30" craft wires. Coil and loop first wire to desired choker size. Repeat for other wire wrapping around first. Wrap a loop at both ends to secure. • Dip into Sulfur then Baking Soda solution (see page 17).

Pendant: Sand Copper lightly and cut to ⅞" x 1¾" for pendant. Round off corners. • Follow instructions on page 17 for stamping with Liver of Sulfur to apply image to metal. Lightly buff edges with steel wool. • Punch hole in center top, side and bottom. Coil and curl Copper craft wire to fit one side of the pendant. Hammer slightly and dip into Liver of Sulfur. Attach to pendant by sewing a small piece of wire through the pendant holes. • Die cut frame from Pewter metal. Texturize as desired. Glue acetate to back of frame. Add photo. Adhere frame and charms to front of pendant as desired. Add beads to head pins and eye pins, then attach to coils.
• Attach pendant to center of choker.

Easy Earrings

Make a fashion statement with earrings that are uniquely yours.

SIZE: ⅝" x 1¾"

MATERIALS:
WireForm (Copper 24 gauge craft wire, thin Copper rods) • Assorted beads and spacers • 2 Silver head pins • Jump rings • Ear wires

INSTRUCTIONS:
Square Coil Earrings: Create a square coil. Loop at top. String beads onto head pin. Attach to coil. Attach earring wire with jump rings.

Drop Earrings: Coil Copper craft wire, loop at top to secure. • Coil dangle: Cut 4" craft wire. Coil one end, shape zigzags, and turn a loop in the end. • Bead dangle: Wire wrap beads and shape the wire tail into zigzags ending with a wrapped loop.
• Attach dangles to Copper coil. Attach ear wires to Copper coil.

1. **Drop Earrings**: Coil the Copper craft wire. • 2. Coil dangle: Coil one end, shape, and turn a loop. • 3. Bead dangle: Wrap bead. • 4. Shape the wire tail. • 5. **Square Coil Earrings**: Shape the coil and turn a loop in the end. • 6. Thread the beads onto a head pin.

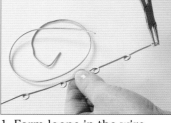

1. Form loops in the wire.

2. Curl the end of the short wire.

3. Hook a short wires onto each loop.

5. Punch holes in Copper.

7. Curl the bracelet into shape.

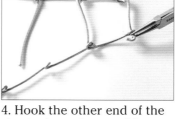

4. Hook the other end of the short wire to its matching loop.

6. Wire Copper to the bracelet.

Aluminum Linked Bracelet

Eclectic, trendy, and definitely one-of-a-kind, this is a good project for using up those leftover scrap pieces of metal.

SIZE: 1¼" x 10"

MATERIALS:
ArtEmboss (Copper, Pewter) • Stencil plastic • WireForm (Aluminum 22 gauge craft wire, ⅛" Aluminum armature wire) • Metal Alphabet stamp set • Metal Stamp pad • Rubber stamps • Black Rub 'n Buff • 1/16" hole punch • Double-sided tape

INSTRUCTIONS:
Cut two 12" pieces of armature wire. Turn a loop at each end. Measure down 1" and create another loop. Repeat until there are 5 loops between the end loops. Loops do not have to be evenly spaced. Repeat these steps on the remaining armature wire, matching the loops as closely as possible. • Cut 7 pieces of armature wire 2½" long. Beginning with 1 looped wire, thread a 2" wire thru a loop.

Bend around loop to secure. Repeat for all short wires. Attach the loose ends to the second looped wire forming rungs of a ladder. • Cut Copper shapes to fit between the ladder rungs. Stamp with desired patterns. • Cut desired shape from stencil plastic. Apply double-sided tape to top. Apply Pewter metal and cut out. Repeat for back side. Texture as desired. Hammer word or phrase into Pewter. Apply Rub 'n Buff to highlight. • Punch holes into Copper and Pewter pieces.

Secure between the ladder rungs by wrapping wire through the hole and around the armature wire. • Mold bracelet to wrist.

Tropicana Necklace

This pendant is the perfect way to dress up a necklace purchased at a dollar store. The original focal pendant was not that attractive, but the necklace was nice – look for potential when buying jewelry.

SIZE: Necklace: 16", Pendant: 3¼" x 3¼"

MATERIALS:
ArtEmboss Pewter • Clear stencil plastic • Copper 24 gauge Fun Wire • WireForm Aluminum craft wire • Wood stylus • Fimo Gel • Seed beads • Pearl Ex Powders (True Blue, Reflex Violet, Duo Blue-Green) • Toothpicks • Paper plate • Heat gun • Double-sided tape • 2 part epoxy glue

INSTRUCTIONS:
Cut 5 petal shapes from plastic using pattern. Apply tape to one side. Cut three pieces of FunWire 2" long. Loop wire at one end. Position wires on petal as shown on pattern. Cut off excess.

Place petal sticky side down onto Pewter. Cut out flush with edges. Burnish metal down onto tape with stylus. Apply tape to back. Apply to metal and cut out.

For each Pearl Ex powder color, pour a quarter size pool of Fimo gel onto a paper plate. Add ⅛ teaspoon Pearl Ex powder. Stir with a toothpick and use the toothpick to paint the gel onto the petal. Begin with light colors and work to dark edges.

Streak colors together with toothpick. Set with heat gun, making sure to keep the heat gun moving. The gel will turn cloudy before it is crystal clear. If the gel is not clear or is milky looking, it is not totally heat set. • Arrange all petals and glue together. Let dry.

Add seed beads to a 6" piece of craft wire. Wrap around finger to create loops Glue loops to center of petal. Let dry. • Cut a strip of metal 1½" x 4". Fold edges into center. Press flat with stylus. Cut it in half. Glue one strip to the back of the flower.

Wrap the other strip around the necklace to gauge the size. Glue to maintain the shape. Remove from necklace and glue loop to back of flower. Let dry. • Bend petals to form a pleasing shape.

1. Adhere looped wire to the petal. • 2. Place petal sticky side down on Pewter. • 3. Burnish metal to bring the wire design to the surface. • 4. Paint the petals.

5. Heat set. • 6. Fold the metal strip and flatten with a stylus. • 7. Glue metal strip to the back of the flower.

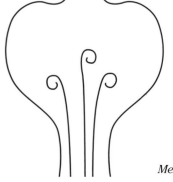

Create a Beautiful Colored Pendant!

Creating Tube Beads with Metal and Wire

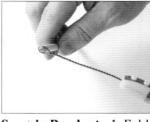

Sangria Pendant - 1. Fold wire in half and twist.

2. Press coiled wire onto tape.

3. Daub project with alcohol inks.

4. Clip the corners of the Pewter.

5. Fold Pewter to the back side and burnish with a stylus.

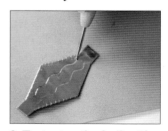

6. Texturize the bail with a metal stylus.

Raindrops Necklace

Fun, flowing, and whimsical, this sparkling necklace is a must-have for every wardrobe. Try a variety of bead sizes and colors for a new look.

SIZE: 20"

MATERIALS:
ArtEmboss Cerulean Blue Aluminum • ¼" Clear plastic tubing used for plumbing refrigerators • Clear stencil plastic • Craft foam • Texture Sheet or plastic Aida cloth • Pasta machine • Silver non-tarnish 18 gauge wire • Silver loops (eight ½", three 1", one 1½") • Chain • 14 Silver ¼" jump rings • Toggle • Round punches (¹⁄₁₆", ⁵⁄₁₆") • Scissors • Double-sided tape (flat sheet, ⅛" wide)

INSTRUCTIONS:
Creating the tube beads: Texturize metal by rolling a sandwich of craft foam, metal and Aida cloth or Texture Sheet through the second thinnest setting of the pasta machine. • Cut tubing into ⅞" sections. Wrap each tube with double-sided tape. • Cut metal into ⅞" widths. Wrap around tubing, overlapping ⅛" and trim. Apply ⅛" strip of tape to overlap end and press down to secure. Apply metal to a 3" square of stencil plastic on one side only. Apply tape only to back side. Punch a ¹⁄₁₆" hole in the template plastic. Center the ⁵⁄₁₆" punch over the hole and punch out circle. Make 10. Peel off tape backing and place a circle on the top and bottom of tube.
• Working off the spool, thread wire thru one hole and out the other end. Create a loop. Create another loop at opposite end. Wrap wire around loop and around bead as desired. • Repeat for a total of 5 beads.

Necklace: Attach 4 beads to Silver ½" loops with jump rings. Attach a 1½" and a 1" Silver loop to the center of the chain with a jump ring. Attach a bead to the large Silver loop with a jump ring. Attach a bead on each side of the center loop. Attach a 1" and a ½" Silver loop on each side with a jump ring. Attach the last two beads, one one each side. Attach a small Silver loop on each side. Attach toggle with jump rings (see page 6).

Raindrops - 1. Layer foam, metal (Blue side up), & Aida or texture sheet. • **2.** Run through pasta machine on second thinnest setting. • **3.** Sand to reveal the pattern. • **4.** Cut ⅞" tubing sections.

5. Wrap tube with metal. Tape the end. • 6. Punch a ¹⁄₁₆" hole in the center of a ⁵⁄₁₆" metal circle.
7. Tape the circle to the end of the bead. • 8. Join Silver loops with a jump ring.

Dog Tag Necklaces

These necklaces are beautifully simple and fast to make. They are also easy to personalize and make great gifts!

SIZE: Necklace: 20", Pendant: 1" x 2¼"

MATERIALS:

ArtEmboss Pewter • Black Rub 'n Buff • Assorted themed charms • Chain • Jump rings • Alphabet metal stamps • Hammer • Clear stencil plastic • Punches (Corner rounder, 1/16" round) • Makeup sponge • Double-sided tape • 2 part epoxy glue

INSTRUCTIONS:

Create rectangles from plastic using pattern and round the corners. Apply double-sided tape to one side of the plastic and adhere Pewter. Cut out flush with sides. Repeat for back side. • Using metal stamp set, hammer in desired word or phrase. Add texture as desired.

Apply Rub 'n Buff with a make up sponge. Let dry, gently buff off leaving Black in the cracks. Glue on charms.

Punch a hole, add a jump ring and thread onto chain. If desired, punch a hole in the bottom and add a jump ring. Attach dangling charms.

Metal Stamping

1. Apply Rub 'n Buff to stamped pendant.
2. Adhere charms to pendant.

Dog Tag Patterns

Sangria Pendant

Embedded wires swirl in an enamel pool surrounded by twisted wire, giving this fabulous pendant a distinctive old world style.

SIZE: Necklace 18", Pendant 2¼" x 2¾"

MATERIALS:

ArtEmboss (Copper Light, Pewter) • Clear stencil plastic • Copper 24 gauge Fun Wire • Wooden stylus • Fimo Gel • Piñata inks • Toothpicks • Make up sponges • Clasp • Jump rings • Leather cording • Heat gun • Double-sided tape • 2 part epoxy glue

INSTRUCTIONS:

Prep: Cut 24" of wire, fold in half and twist together. • Cut out pendant patterns from plastic and apply tape to the top of both pieces.

Top pattern: Outline edges with twisted wire. Create coils from Fun Wire and apply to design. Cover with Copper. Burnish metal to tape, going around all edges and rubbing over twisted wire to highlight design. Cut out leaving a ¼" border. Fold edges to back. Apply alcohol ink to the front in desired colors. Apply Clear Fimo gel to surface and heat set.

Bottom layer: Adhere Pewter metal to the top of the large backing piece. Cut out leaving a ¼" border. Clip the corners. Fold over to back side.

Bail: Cut 2 pieces of Pewter 1" x 2½". Tape metal pieces together for double thickness. Using a stylus, trace the bail pattern onto the metal. Apply texture to bail as desired. Cut out. Apply tape to tabs. Peel off tape backing to expose adhesive on bail tabs. Fold around stylus to shape bail and press onto metal square. One tab goes on the front, one tab goes on the back. Apply tape to the back of pewter piece and lay onto Pewter metal. Cut out close to edge. Use stylus to smooth edges.

Necklace: Glue top layer to bottom layer. Let dry. String onto leather cording. Attach cording to clasp with jump rings.

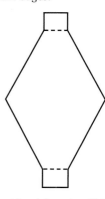

Indian Summer Arrowhead Jewelry

Turquoise and copper always bring to mind the great Southwest and its rich history. Step back in time with this rustic Arrowhead pendant.

SIZE: Necklace 20", Pendant 2½" x 3¾"

MATERIALS:
ArtEmboss Copper Light • WireForm (Copper craft wire, thin Copper rod) • Liver of Sulfur • Baking soda • Turquoise donut bead • Black bead • Small disk beads • S-clasp • Leather cording • Twig

INSTRUCTIONS:
Prep: Dip Copper into Liver of Sulfur solution (page 17). Highlight with steel wool.
Wrap the twig: Cut 3" of twig. Wrap with Copper metal. Wrap craft wire around twig in center leaving a long tail for attaching the Black bead.
Necklace: Wire wrap the Black bead. Using the tail from wrapping the twig, thread wire through the middle wrapping on the bead. Wrap wire end around the twig. • Thread leather cord through one end of the bead, fold in half and wrap with wire to secure. Repeat for the other side. • Add S-clasp.
Wire wrap disk bead: Thread wire thru hole in disk bead, over the top and back thru

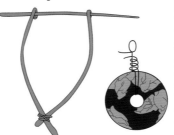

hole. Repeat. Wrap the ends of one wire around the top. Create a loop close to the bead with opposite wire and wrap end around until wire is gone and has formed a coil on the bead.
Arrowhead: Cut Copper rods: 2¾", 3", 3½". • Create a loop at one end of the 3" and 3½" rods. Hammer opposite ends flat. Slightly curve. Thread straight rod thru one loop, the disk bead loop and the loop of the other curved rod. Wire wrap bottom where two rods come together to form a point. • Attach arrowhead pendant to stick by wrapping each end with wire.

1. Wrap wire around Copper covered stick. • 2. Thread wire tail through the middle of the wire wrapped bead. • 3. Thread leather cord through one end of the wrapped bead, fold and wrap with wire to secure. • 4. Wrap wire around the top of the donut. • 5. Hook the bent rod onto the flat rod.

Copper Flower Pendant

Flowers have inspired metal craftsmen to fashion sensational pieces. Create a pendant featuring your favorite floral. Metal stencils make it easy for you to fashion something beautiful.

SIZE: Necklace 18", Pendant 2½" x 2½"

MATERIALS:
ArtEmboss (Copper Light, Pewter) • 4 WireForm thin Copper rods • Copper craft wire • 2 Copper eyelets • Liver of Sulfur • Baking Soda • Floral Embossing Template • Stencil plastic • Wooden stylus • Craft foam • Make up sponge • Black Rub 'n Buff • Steel wool • Tub of water • Eyelet tools • ⅛" round punch • Rubber mallet • Double-sided tape • Hot glue gun

INSTRUCTIONS:
Prep: Follow instructions on page 17 for using Liver of Sulfur to tarnish and darken metal. Dip all the brass rods as well as the spool of Copper wire into Sulfur solution.
Pendant: Use the craft foam as a base to emboss the Copper. Lay template onto Copper and emboss with wooden stylus. Keep working the metal gently so that it stretches and creates a deep impression. Using steel wool, gently buff the surface to reveal the bright Copper embossed areas. Cut out to desired size square. Apply tape to entire back side. • Measure Copper square and add ¼" to each side. Cut this size square out of stencil plastic and cover both sides with tape. Round corners. Adhere a piece of Pewter to the back and trim to fit. • Glue dots onto rubber mallet with glue gun and pound a sheet of Pewter to texturize it. Use steel wool to rough. Apply Black Rub 'n Buff. Let dry slightly and buff off leaving as much as

continued on page 14

. Stack foam, metal and stencil.
Use heavy pressure to emboss
stencil deeply.

. Gently buff raised areas of the
esign with steel wool.

Adhere foam dots to the mallet
nd strike Pewter to texturize.

Apply Rub 'n Buff to the metal.

Wrap choker wires together.

Coil the ends of the short chok-
 wires.

Wrap the tail of the short wires
d trim as needed.

Shape clasp pieces.

Sea Gypsy Ensemble

Capture the freedom of a Sea Gypsy as bubbles and waves dance across a sea green and aqua enameled ensemble.

SIZE: Necklace 20"
            Pendant 2½" x 2½"
            Earrings: 1¾" x 1¾"

MATERIALS:
ArtEmboss Pewter • Fun Wire
• WireForm Aluminum craft wire
• Wood stylus • Fimo Gel • Clear template plastic • Pearl Ex Powders (Reflex Violet, Duo Blue-Green, Duo Green-Yellow) • Jump rings • Silver hoops (1" for pendant, two ½" for earrings) • Decorative chain
• Lobster claw clasp • Ear wires
• Silver non-tarnish 22 gauge wire
• Heat gun • Double-sided tape
• 2 part epoxy glue

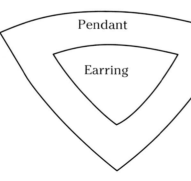

Pendant

Earring

INSTRUCTIONS:
Pendant: Cut pattern from plastic. Apply double-sided tape to front. Create shapes with Fun Wire and press onto tape. Adhere jump rings. Cover pendant with Pewter. Trim leaving a ¼" border. Fold edges to the back. On right side, use a stylus to burnish metal to reveal pattern.
• Apply tape to back of design. Add a large Silver loop at the top. Coil a 2" piece of wire on one end, zig-zag and finish with loop. Adhere at bottom and cover with Pewter. Cut out flush. Smooth edges with stylus.
• Mix Pearl Ex powder into Fimo Gel. On the front of the project, paint into crevasses. Set with heat gun. • Attach pendant to chain with jump rings and add clasp.
Earrings: Follow pendant directions using the pattern for the earrings. Attach loops to ear wires.

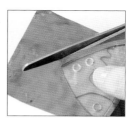

Enameled Jewelry

1. Adhere Fun Wire shapes and jump rings to pendant. • 2. Cover pendant with Pewter. • 3. Trim leaving a ¼" border.

4. Fold edges to the back. • 5. Turn project to the front and burnish with a stylus. • 6. Adhere Silver loop and wire swirl to the back of the project. Cover back with Pewter.

Copper Flower Pendant – INSTRUCTIONS continued from page 12: desired in grooves. Adhere textured Pewter to tape on the front of plastic square and trim leaving a ⅛" border. Clip edges and fold to back. Burnish edges with wooden stylus. Adhere Copper embossed flower to center of pewter square. • Punch a hole in each upper corner and set an eyelet. • Attach Copper wire with loop, twist wire and finish with loop.

Choker: Use 2 full size lengths of Copper rods. Loop each end. Wrap rods together with loops going in opposite directions. • Fold Copper rod in half. Coil one of the ends and wrap the remaining end near the coil to finish. • Repeat for wire on the other side. Shape clasps from 2 pieces of 5" Copper rod. Attach ends with jump rings made from rods. See instructions for making jump rings on page 6.

SIZE: Necklace: 19"
Pendant: 3" x 3"
MATERIALS:
ArtEmboss Copper medium • WireForm thin Copper rod • Wooden stylus • Fimo Gel • Piñata alcohol inks (Santa Fe Red, Calabaza Orange, Havana Brown) • Rubbing Alcohol • Make up sponges • Toothpicks • Heat gun • Double-sided tape • 2 part epoxy glue
INSTRUCTIONS:
Leaf: Apply double-sided tape to Copper to create a double thickness. Cut out leaf pattern. Smooth edges and draw veins with stylus. Daub ink onto metal surface in an irregular pattern. Spritz with alcohol. Apply Clear gel over top of leaf. Heat set.
Tendril: Bend wire in half by folding it over a pencil. Coil one end of brass rod and then zig-zag. Fold end of wire down and around, finishing with a loose coil. Glue coil onto top of pendant. Let dry. Bend remaining wire into a pleasing shape. Add to purchased necklace.

1. Draw veins with a metal stylus.

2. Daub alcohol inks onto metal.

3. Fold the wire in half over a pencil.

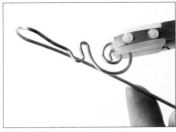

4. Coil one end and shape a zigzag.

5. Create a loop.

Autumn Leaf Pendant
Resplendent with the textures of Autumn, this stunning pendant enhances your accessory wardrobe with the warm colors of fall.

Simulated Silver Pendants

Pewter metal is great for simulating the look of a Silver pendant. Begin with simple straight-line shapes that are easier to cover with metal. As you progress, you can work your way into oval and more rounded shapes.

Attach small square shapes together for an attractive coordinating bracelet.

SIZE: Necklace: 18"   Triangle Pendant: 1¾" x 2"
Rectangle Pendant: ¾" x 1¾"

MATERIALS:
ArtEmboss Pewter • Friendly Plastic • Polyblade • Friendly cutters (small circle shapes) • Stencil plastic • Silver loops • Chain • Aluminum foil • Baby oil • Heat gun • Bowl of cold water • Double-sided tape

INSTRUCTIONS:
Rub baby oil on hands to help prevent plastic from sticking to skin. Also lightly coat aluminum foil with oil.

Friendly plastic focal piece: Cut pieces from pattern. Stack pieces following the diagram and place onto aluminum foil. Heat with heat gun. The plastic will get very gooey the hotter it gets. Do not touch with fingers as it will burn and also leave finger prints. Once plastic is melted together, immediately immerse the aluminum foil into cold water to harden. Peel design from foil. Trim edges if needed. Apply double-sided tape to back side.

Faux Silver Settings – Focal Pendants

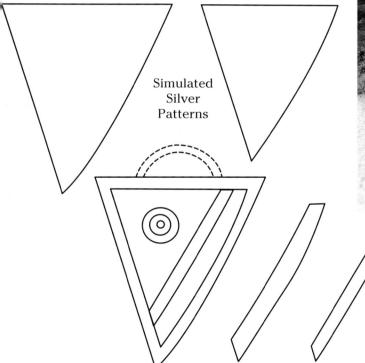

Simulated Silver Patterns

Background: Use background pattern to trace triangle onto plastic. Apply tape to front. Lay face down onto Pewter and cut out leaving ⅛" border. Clip corners. Fold edges to back and burnish with a wood stylus. Draw texture lines along the front edge with a metal stylus. Apply tape to back. Add Silver loop. Lay sticky side down onto metal and cut out flush. Burnish edges and around loop with wood stylus.

Finish: Peel backing from tape on the focal piece and adhere to the background. Attach a jump ring to the loop and thread onto a chain.

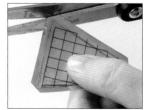
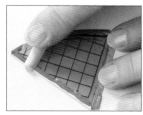

1. Stack Friendly Plastic pieces on aluminum foil and melt with a heat gun. • 2. Clip the corners so the edges are easier to fold to the back. • 3. Burnish the folded edges. • 4. Draw texture lines along the front edge. • 5. Adhere the plastic piece to the background.

Organic Treasures

Distinctive curls and wraps combine with natural stone for an exotic and organic style.

SIZE: Necklace: 16"   Pendant: 2" x 4"
             Bracelet: 1½" x 8"   Earrings: 1½" x 3"

MATERIALS:
WireForm (thin Copper rods, Copper 24 gauge craft wire) • Liver of Sulfur • Baking Soda • Disk beads • Assorted beads • Leather cording • Hammer • Bamboo skewer • 3" twig for earrings

INSTRUCTIONS:

Pendant: Cut rods into the following lengths: 2", 2½", 4", and 6". See Assembly Diagram for placement of the pieces. • Turn a loop in the top of the 2½" center piece as shown in the Diagram. Thread on disk bead. Turn a loop in the bottom. • Create 4" and 6" side pieces, hammer flat and attach following the Assembly Diagram. • Wrap craft wire around a bamboo skewer to create a coil. Slightly pull apart and thread onto straight craft wire. Attach to side following the Assembly Diagram. Wrap additional craft wire around side piece as desired. • Hammer 2" piece and attach at top by wrapping with Copper craft wire. • Attach beads as dangles to bottom.

Necklace: Cut a 5" rod. See Assembly Diagram . • Thread the rod through the loop at the top of the center wire. Wrap with craft wire. Loop ends. Tie leather cording to each end in length desired. Dip into Liver of Sulfur and Baking Soda solution. Buff with steel wool to highlight and shine. • Create an S-clasp. Attach leather to clasp.

Earrings: Cut rods 1", 1¾" and 3". Cut a ¾" twig for each earring. See photo for placement of the pieces. • Turn a loop in the top of the 1¾" center piece as shown in the Diagram. Thread on disk bead. Turn a loop in the bottom. • Create 3" side piece, hammer flat and attach following the Assembly Diagram. • Wrap craft wire around a 1" flattened Copper rod and attach to the side piece as a dangle. On the right side, wrap a small bead and attach to the side piece as a dangle. On the right side, wrap a small bead and attach with craft wire. Add a beaded dangle to the bottom loop of the center rod. Attach the twig above the donut bead with craft wire Attach ear wire to top loop.

Bracelet: Gather leftover beads. Follow directions for necklace pendant, replacing the coil with a loop. Bend a Copper rod in half. Randomly zig-zag each side ending in a coil. Attach coils to center pendant by wrapping with Copper craft wire. Add beads between loops as desired. Repeat for other side. Create clasp to secure to wrist. Adjust by pinching zig zag together.

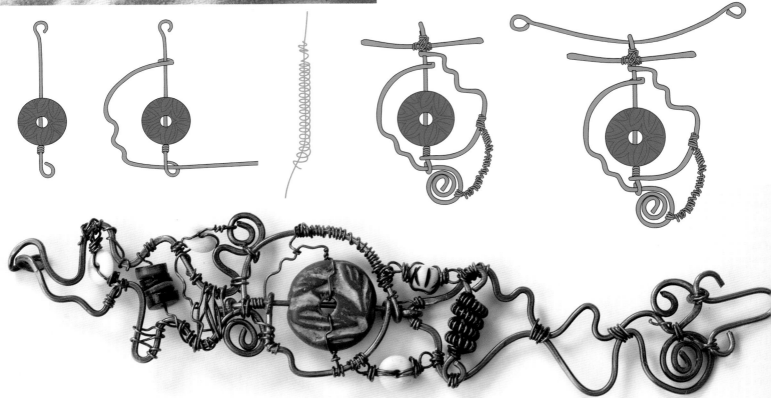

USING LIVER OF SULFUR

GENERAL INSTRUCTIONS:

Liver of Sulfur comes in small pebble shapes that are not the same size. The larger the chunk you use, the faster the metal will turn colors and the less control you have over the intensity. I recommend using a pea size amount in hot water.

Dissolve 2 Tablespoons Baking Soda in another bowl of water.

Have all pieces ready to dip. Make sure that you are in a well ventilated area as it is quite smelly.

Using a pair of tweezers, dip Copper into Sulfur solution. Then dip into Baking Soda to stop the oxidation process. Buff with steel wool to highlight.

Time saving tip: Dip the entire spool of Copper craft wire. It may oxidize and become White. Simply wipe with steel wool to brighten and clean. I also dip several extra pieces of Copper while I have the solution ready to go.

STAMPING WITH LIVER OF SULFUR

Use a half-pea size bit of Sulfur and dissolve it in cool tap water. If the water is too hot, it will melt away the petroleum jelly and will result in a mottled, distorted image.

Dissolve 2 Tablespoons Baking Soda in another bowl of water.

Apply a very light coat of petroleum jelly to rubber stamp. Stamp images onto prepared metal.

Dip into Liver of Sulfur solution to expose pattern, then dip into Baking Soda solution.

Wipe away petroleum jelly with a paper towel.

Links & Kinks Necklace

This intriguing necklace is fun and random. Adjust the length by adding or removing coils.

SIZE: 33"

MATERIALS: WireForm (Copper craft wire, Thin Copper rods) • Liver of Sulfur • Baking Soda • Assorted beads (Disk, large bi-cone, round)

INSTRUCTIONS:

Prep: Dip all wire into Liver of Sulfur solution before beginning. • Curl and coil randomly several lengths of Copper rod.

Hand: Cut 15" of Copper rod. Create a coil in one end. Bend the rod following pattern and end with a loop.

Center Spiral: Cut 6" of rod, bend in half. Coil ends around. Finish with loop.

Beads: Cut 9" of Copper craft wire. At one end, form a wrapped loop. Thread Copper craft wire through beads and wrap a loop. Wrap the tail around beads. Add little zigzags with pliers if desired.

Finish: Attach beads to rods at loop. Use pliers to close loop completely. Add a toggle if desired or make the necklace long enough to fit over your head.

1. Hand: Coil the end and shape following pattern. • 2. Center Spiral: Fold rod in half and begin coil. • 3. Continue shaping spiral. • 4. Turn a loop in the end.

5. Shape random curves for connector pieces. • 6. Make a wrapped loop in one end of a Copper wire. • 7. Thread beads. • 8. Form another wrapped loop and wrap the tail around the beads.

SIZE: Necklace: 20"
      Pendant: 1¾" x 2½"
      Bracelet: 1¼" x 8"

MATERIALS:
ArtEmboss (Copper Medium, Pewter) • WireForm (Copper craft wire, thin Copper rod) • Liver of Sulfur • Baking Soda • Clear aceta[t] • Rub 'n Buff • Photos • Eyelets • Assorted beads • Charms • Jum[p] rings • Findings • Clasps • Leather cording • Big Kick Die Cut machine • Sizzix die cut Gelly-O 1¼" square frame • Rubber stamp • Petroleu[m] jelly • 220 grit sandpaper • Steel wool • Eyelet tools • Punches (1⁹⁄₁₆" square, 2" square, Corner rounder) • *We R Memory Keepers* Crop-A-Dile punch • Double-sided tape • 2 part epoxy glue

INSTRUCTIONS:

Prep: See instructions for Stampin[g] with Liver of Sulfur on page 17.

Copper backing: Sand metal. • Apply a very thin layer of petrole[u]m jelly to rubber stamp. Stamp images onto Copper. Dip into Live[r] of Sulfur and then into Baking Sod[a] solution. • Punch out two 1⁹⁄₁₆" squares. Lightly buff edges with steel wool to polish and highlight. Tape squares back to back alignin[g] edges. Round corners. Punch a ⅛" hole in top center. Set eyelet. Adhere metal charm.

Photo frame: Apply tape to both sides of a 2" square of stencil plas[t]ic. Remove backing and apply Pewter metal to one side. Die cut frame. Texturize metal as desired and antique with Rub 'n Buff. Remove backing and center frame over photo. Stamp word onto metal. Cut out and glue to front of photo. Apply tape to back of phot[o] and apply Copper metal. Trim edges even. Use a wooden stylus t[o] smooth any rough metal edges. Se[t] eyelets in each frame hole. • Add charms and beaded dangles to bo[t]tom of photo frame.

Necklace: Coil each end of a 4" piece of Copper rod. Wrap with craft wire. Wrap again, this time, creating a loop in center for attach[]ing the pendant. Attach pendant layers with a jump ring. • Wrap wire around end of leather cordin[g] leaving a 2" tail. Thread end thru coil and wrap remaining wire around coil to secure. Trim if need[]ed. Repeat for opposite side.

Bracelet: Follow directions for the photo frame. Glue themed charm[s] and words to photo and frame if desired. Join frames with jump rings. • Thread beads onto head pins and attach to the jump rings between the frames to create dan[]gles. Attach clasp to each end.

Made for Memories Necklace and Bracelet

Specially designed to please everyone who loves combining photos and charms with wearable art, this Memory ensemble is going to be a favorite with family and friends.

1. Sand the Copper metal. • 2. Apply a thin coat of petroleum jelly to the stamp. • 3. Stamp the image onto Copper. • 4. Dip the stamped metal into Liver of Sulfur, then Baking Soda solution.

5. Punch a ⅛" hole in the Copper square with a Crop-a-Dile tool. • 6. Curl the end of the Copper rod. • 7. Wrap wire around the rod. • 8. Thread wire tail through the center of the swirl and wrap to secure.

9. Trim acetate even with the frame. • 10. Position photo under frame and trim to fit. • 11. Attach dangles to bottom of frame with a jump ring. • 12. Attach frame to Copper background with a jump ring.